Call Me Madame

Martina Devlin

Call Me Madame

ARLEN HOUSE

Call Me Madame

is published in 2022 by
ARLEN HOUSE
42 Grange Abbey Road
Baldoyle, Dublin 13
Ireland
Email: arlenhouse@gmail.com
www.arlenhouse.ie

ISBN 978–1–85132–282–4, paperback

International distribution
SYRACUSE UNIVERSITY PRESS
621 Skytop Road, Suite 110
Syracuse
New York 13244–5290
USA
Email: supress@syr.edu
www.syracuseuniversitypress.syr.edu

Typesetting by Arlen House

cover image: courtesy of Mícheál Ó Doibhilín,
designer and publisher of Kilmainham Tales Teo.

arts council of Northern Ireland

LOTTERY FUNDED

CONTENTS

Introduction

My father led me to Countess Markievicz. One Sunday, our family of seven children was jammed into the car for the sixty-mile trip (we didn't count in kilometres then) to Lissadell House in Sligo. At that time, you could only walk through some of the grounds because the house was private, occupied still by Gore-Booths, but it was impossible to miss the imposing grey property with its "Great windows open to the south," as W.B. Yeats immortalises it.[1] I remember peeping through foliage, overawed, as any eight-year-old would be. "A right barracks of a place," agreed my parents, while admiring its curved limestone facade; and, indeed, it was austere, impassive and rather ramshackle – yet with an undeniable magnificence. As we children darted about, shaking out our limbs after the journey, my father told us snippets about the rebel countess and her remarkable life. Captivated, I shadowed him, a freckled small mass of questions.

Decades passed, and it was 2018. My collection of short stories was published, *Truth & Dare: Short Stories about*

Women who Shaped Ireland, with one about Countess Markievicz among them, 'What Would the Countess Say?'[2] I had never forgotten her, or Lissadell. When I decided to retrieve some of the countless sidelined women of note from our collective amnesia, she was uppermost on my list. Unlike many, she is remembered, but narrowly – as a leader in the Easter Rising. The full panoply of her career is often glossed over. That short story was an attempt to breathe life – and fun – into a contradictory character who was both aristocrat and republican, revolutionary and politician.

Constance Gore-Booth, later Countess Markievicz, was born in 1868 to Arctic explorer and landlord Sir Henry Gore-Booth, and Georgina Hill of Yorkshire, niece to the Earl of Scarborough. The family produced two exceptional women: not just Constance, or Con, but her younger sister, Eva, a prominent labour rights campaigner and poet. Lissadell was their Irish seat, but the Gore-Booths owned homes in Dublin and London, where the future countess was born. If life is "more like wrestling than dancing" as a Stoic philosopher puts it, then Countess Markievicz did her fair share of the former. There must have been some time set aside for dancing in her youth because she was a debutante, presented to Queen Victoria. However, the wrestling – activism, plotting, fighting and politicking – monopolised her attention.

She was also a talented artist, studying at The Slade in London and in Paris, where she met her husband, Casimir Dunin Markievicz, known as Count Markievicz, who had estates in Ukraine. They settled in Dublin in the early 1900s, where, from 1908, she became embedded in nationalist politics while her husband gravitated toward set design for the Abbey Theatre. She could have embraced the genteel life of a society lady, or the bohemian life of an artist with private means. Instead, she was drawn to issues around social justice, and fired in the crucible of revolutionary politics.

Every schoolchild learns how she was condemned to face a firing squad after the Rising, in which she served as an office in James Connolly's Irish Citizen Army, but her sentence was remitted to penal servitude for life. Unusually, the countess challenged her reprieve. In her own words, in a newspaper interview in June 1917 following her release from prison in Aylesbury:

> ... as I was standing on the table looking out of the window of my cell, an officer came in and read my death sentence to me twice, and then added that it had been commuted to penal servitude for life. I said, 'I wish you had the decency to shoot me.'[3]

From anyone else it might sound like grandstanding, from the countess it is utterly credible.

When I decided to write about her, the role she played in revolution interested me less than her social activism. What gave this high-born hybrid her empathy with the populace? What drove her to push for all manner of ground-breaking freedoms for people, from equality between women and men, to class barriers torn down, to labour rights for workers? With that in mind, I raised her from the dead to cast a cold eye on present-day Ireland, and the glacial pace of political reform. The following year, the story had a new lease of life as a play staged to commemorate the centenary of her appointment as first female Cabinet member in the fledgling Irish State.

When the inaugural Dáil Éireann met in 1919 while she was in jail, she was not only its first female TD, but was given the Minister for Labour portfolio. Consequently, she was the first female government minister in a modern democracy – second in the world, behind Russia. It would be sixty years before another woman held a ministry in the Dáil. Sometimes, when you recite the detail of those mountains she climbed, the numbing hand of history paralyses it. But it was an extraordinary feat.

Every performance of a playwright's work is magical, but the one which pleased me best was held in 2019 by invitation of the Lord Mayor of Dublin, in the Round Room of the Mansion House. That venue was the location of the first Dáil, and it felt right to tell some element of her story there. At every presentation of the play, audience members waited behind to share their family memories of encounters with her, and I realised how greatly she had been loved – and remained loved.

At a performance in Dalkey Castle & Heritage Centre, an elderly woman approached me to say the countess had painted her mother as a girl of nineteen or so, when they were jailed together in the North Dublin Union. The portrait was hanging in her home – would I like to see it? Of course! A visit was arranged, and I viewed a small painting of a pretty, dark-haired girl sitting at a table in a prison cell, chin on her hand. It was signed Constance de Markievicz, dated December 1923, and showed her to be a talented artist. In a typical act of generosity, the countess gave the portrait to her sitter – she treasured it, and passed it on to her daughter as an heirloom. As I peered at the brush strokes, I recalled how the countess – always resourceful – collected feathers in the prison exercise yard for her artwork.

My hostess spoke about her mother's admiration for the countess, who was addressed as Madame in a nod to the French revolution (pronounced madam), and the key message I took away was that she was kind and plucky. Her bravery and leadership during confinement inspired the other girls and women who were incarcerated with her, this time by the Free State government cracking down on those who opposed the Anglo-Irish Treaty. The countess's own class regarded her as having gone rogue, but the people saw it differently, appreciating her advocacy for workers. Clearly, she could be maddening at times. Kathleen Clarke obviously thought so, complaining about her endless talking when they were cellmates. Her energy and confidence must have been contagious – except when they proved overwhelming.

Countess Markievicz was the first woman elected to the House of Commons in the 1918 general election, but did not take her seat, in line with her Sinn Féin party's abstentionism. To mark her history-making status, in 2018 the 1916 Relatives Association had a series of posters erected on Dublin lamp posts, designed by Mícheál Ó Doibhilín, which quickly became collectors' items. Some were even pinched from their lofty perch! Courtesy of the association's chair at the time, Brían O'Neill, I was given one as a Christmas present that year, and it has hung in my hall ever since.

The countess's achievement in being elected to the "mother of parliaments" tends to be skimmed over in Britain. To remind MPs, the Oireachtas donated a photographic copy of a 1901 portrait (she looks like an Edwardian socialite rather than a nascent revolutionary) to an exhibition in Westminster. It was to ensure she had a place there, if not a seat.

The best-laid plans etc. After the close of the centenary exhibition about women winning the vote, her portrait was no longer on display, until rescued by Irish-born Labour MP Conor McGinn, who scooped her up to hang in his office. When I found myself in London on business, I trooped off to his rooms to admire her virtual presence in parliament buildings of the state she took arms against. Suitable to its surroundings though the portrait was, I indulged in a reverie whereby the Oireachtas had offered an image representing her in another incarnation. In 1914, during a suffrage extravaganza at Molesworth Hall in

Dublin, the countess had dressed up as Joan of Arc in painted cardboard armour, cutting a dramatic figure. Imagine how striking an artist's version of those photographs would have been! In any event, thanks to Conor McGinn's intercession, Constance de Markievicz's portrait is now part of a permanent exhibition on women's suffrage near the public gallery for the House of Commons' chamber.

On that same trip to London, I went looking for the house where she was born, along with some friends – we found it at Buckingham Gate, a stone's throw from Buckingham Palace. The three of us gave ourselves cricks in the neck gazing up, up, upwards at its elegant heights. There was no doubting the countess sprang from wealth and privilege, although she gave away most of her money.

The trajectory of her life reveals how she found meaning through the nationalist cause, as well as the intertwined struggle for workers' and women's rights – on the latter issue, she was quick to recognise the vote as an important political weapon. But such facts don't necessarily reveal the person behind them. Similarly, her face in photographs, whether wearing jewels, or in uniform, or stroking her dog Poppet, give us some insight into the countess – but not the whole story. Perhaps we come closest to understanding her when we hear her voice through letters and newspaper articles, which showcase her wit and idealism. In one piece, she urged women not to trust to their feminine charm, which meant relying on the problematic chivalry of men, but to depend on themselves. Elsewhere, she spoke of the need to cultivate the masculine side of women's souls and feminine side of men's, which sounds a modern note – yet she was advocating it more than a century ago.

Countess Markievicz doesn't convince as one of life's compromisers, but revolution eventually gave way to constitutional politics, although a Dáil exchange with Michael Collins demonstrates how venomous the relationship between former comrades became after independence. The republican movement split over partition and Free State status, needling her to shout "traitor" at Collins while he yelled "English" at her in an unedifying tit-for-tat exchange. Nevertheless, she transitioned to the political mainstream as a founding member of Fianna Fáil, and was elected a TD of the new party just weeks before she died.

Repeated prison terms – she served time in five different jails in Ireland and England – in addition to periods on the run and on hunger strike, ground down her health. By the time she died in 1927, in the public ward of a hospital where she wanted to be, she looked years older. No longer was she one of those "Two girls in silk kimonos, both/Beautiful, one a gazelle" about whom W.B. Yeats had been moved to devise poetry – it's unlikely she cared.[4] Even so, however ramshackle she became, like Lissadell before it was sold to its current owners, she had that same underlying magnificence. The Cumann na nGaedheal government, her political rivals, denied her a state funeral – no matter, the people turned out in their hordes to give her a de facto one, Dublin at a standstill. While they didn't always see eye to eye, Lady Gregory observed after her death, "There was something gallant about her."[5] That gallantry is obvious in a May 1916 letter to Eva, written in the aftermath of the Rising. "Now darling, don't worry about me, for I'm not too bad at all and it's only a mean spirit that grudges paying the price."[6]

Countess Markievicz's life teaches us there is no necessity in history – events don't happen because they must, but because people bring them about. She belongs to another time, yet her message is a contemporary one: if you believe in something, work to deliver it with every iota of your strength. Some say the countess had a fanatic's heart – I say she had passion, enough to make her unstoppable and unforgettable.

NOTES

1 W.B. Yeats, 'In Memory of Eva Gore-Booth and Con Markievicz' from *The Winding Stair and Other Poems* (London, Macmillan, 1933).

2 Martina Devlin, *Truth & Dare: Short Stories about Women Who Shaped Ireland* (Dublin, Poolbeg Press, 2018).

3 Interview in the *Evening Telegraph*, Dublin, 17 June 1917.

4 Yeats, 'In Memory of Eva Gore-Booth and Con Markievicz', *op. cit.*

5 *Lady Gregory's Journals 1916–1930*, edited by Lennox Robinson (New York, Macmillan, 1947).

6 National Library of Ireland collection, MS 5763/3.

Constance Markievicz, 1917

These posters were put up on Dublin lamp posts in 2018 by the 1916 Relatives Association to mark the centenary of Countess Markievicz's election. Designed by historian and publisher Mícheál Ó Doibhilín of Kilmainham Tales, Teo.

Performance Rights

For permission to perform this play, contact martinadevlinwriter@gmail.com

Performance History

This play was performed three times in 2019, under the title *What Would The Countess Say?*

It went on twice in Dalkey Castle & Heritage Centre, Dublin, with thanks to director Margaret Dunne; and once in the Mansion House, Dublin, with thanks to then Lord Mayor Nial Ring and the Mansion House staff.

Call Me Madame

Characters

Aoife Blanchard, late twenties, eager, wearing jeans.

Countess Markievicz, late fifties, imposing, wearing fitted tweed jacket and skirt that stops just above her ankles.

Security guard, a Jobsworth type, wearing hi-vis waistcoat.

Taoiseach Leo Varadkar, wearing tracksuit.

Setting

Dublin, 2019

ACT ONE

The present day. A first-floor apartment in a redbrick terraced house on the South Circular Road, Dublin.

AOIFE BLANCHARD *enters the living room drinking from a bottle of water. She stops short, splashing water over her t-shirt.*

Another woman is in the room. It is COUNTESS MARKIEVICZ, *wearing a broad-brimmed hat.*

COUNTESS MARKIEVICZ: Kindly stop staring at me, young woman. Don't you know it's rude to stare? *(Pulls off her hat, fans her face).* Could someone please open a window? There's no air in here.

AOIFE *gapes. With a visible effort she recovers her powers of speech.*

AOIFE: Forgive me, I wasn't expecting it to work. Especially not the first time. I've never attempted a materialisation before. But here you are. It is you, isn't it? Countess Markievicz?

Behind the COUNTESS'*s commanding veneer, a faint air of bewilderment is apparent.*

COUNTESS MARKIEVICZ: You are addressing Constance de Markievicz. Have we met?

AOIFE: I'm afraid not. You've been dead for more than ninety years.

COUNTESS MARKIEVICZ: Really, this is too ridiculous. My head's pounding – I can't concentrate. I say, why hasn't anyone opened that window yet?

AOIFE *sets down her plastic bottle and tugs at the sash. As she steps back, the* COUNTESS *holds up a warning hand.*

COUNTESS MARKIEVICZ: Watch out! Don't tread on Poppet!

AOIFE: What's Poppet?

COUNTESS MARKIEVICZ: My dog, of course.

AOIFE: I don't see any dog.

The COUNTESS *checks under the coffee table and peers round the back of the sofa.*

COUNTESS MARKIEVICZ: Oh, Poppet isn't with me. How disappointing. Little scamp's generally at my heels. I wonder where he's taken himself off to? (*Extends her hand).* Since there's no one to introduce us, we must do it ourselves. How do you do?

AOIFE *bobs a curtsey.*

AOIFE: Aoife Blanchard. It's an honour to meet you.

COUNTESS MARKIEVICZ: Why on earth are you genuflecting? Shoulders back! Stand up straight, young woman! The Irish bend the knee to no one.

AOIFE: So sorry, Countess. The etiquette for interacting with titled people isn't one of my strong points.

COUNTESS MARKIEVICZ: No need to stand on ceremony. And you address me as 'Madame' not 'Countess'. (*Tosses hat onto sofa*). Miss Blanchard, I really think you might stop gawping. You look like you've seen a ghost.

AOIFE: But I have, Madame. You're one. A ghost, I mean. I've summoned you up from the dead. I do hope you don't mind. I didn't hold out much hope, to be honest, but it was worth a try. And here you are – just as real as if you're flesh and blood!

COUNTESS MARKIEVICZ: Steady on with the name-calling. Of course I'm real.

AOIFE: Actually, you aren't. I can prove it. What's today's date?

COUNTESS MARKIEVICZ: July the fifteenth 1927.

AOIFE: How interesting. That's the day you died. Rather a long time ago, I'm afraid. Here's today's newspaper.

The date's on the front. See? April the second.

The COUNTESS *takes it between her hands.*

COUNTESS MARKIEVICZ: There's something familiar about that date. I have it! April the second is when I was named Minister for Labour. (*Puffs up*). And a dashed fine one I was, too. If I say so myself. Took no nonsense from anyone.

AOIFE: That was April the second *1919*, Countess – I mean Madame. Look again. It says April the second *2019*.

The COUNTESS *stares at the newspaper, forehead ruffling.*

AOIFE: Look outside. It's a completely different world to the one you knew.

The COUNTESS *crosses to the window, sticks out her head and shoulders, and gasps. Hurriedly, she draws back her upper body into the room.*

COUNTESS MARKIEVICZ: Gracious me, what a lot of motor cars. And they're positively whizzing along! Where are all the horses?

AOIFE: Replaced by the engine.

COUNTESS MARKIEVICZ: No harm, I dare say. Some of the poor beasts were treated abysmally. (*Gazes into space*). I'm finding this rather a lot to take in. I wonder if I'm in the middle of a dream? Could I have eaten something which disagreed with me? I seem to recall a horrid bout of indigestion. And someone saying I was as white as a sheet and ought to see a doctor. Naturally I said I was far too busy. But they're not terribly substantial memories. May I?

She flops into an armchair, plucks at her collar and undoes her top button. AOIFE *walks to a desk in the corner, where a laptop rests. She clicks it into life and taps a few words into a search engine. An image appears on the screen. She carries the laptop to the* COUNTESS.

AOIFE: Look, that's a photograph of your funeral. Here's the newspaper account.

COUNTESS MARKIEVICZ *(agitated, sits bolt upright)*: What is that malevolent-looking object? Remove it at once!

AOIFE: All right, I'll read it to you.

'Large numbers of people marched in the funeral procession of Madame Markievicz, T.D., yesterday afternoon. Several thousands lined the route through the city. A guard of Fianna Éireann boys dressed in green uniforms led the way. They were followed by the brass band of the Irish National Foresters and a detachment of the Citizen Army.

(The COUNTESS *begins to rally, looks over Aoife's shoulder).*

Members of the 1916 Club came next. They carried a floral cross with the inscription 'In Loving Memory of Our Old Comrade'. A big contingent of girls and women represented the Cumann na mBan, the Clan na nGaedheal and the Women's Defence League.'

That's some photograph, Madame. Shows the city at a standstill.

COUNTESS MARKIEVICZ: I must admit, it *is* rather gratifying. (*A neighing laugh).* I'm feeling ridiculously puffed up. Though it's somewhat unsettling to see my funeral there in black and white. Tell me, did Casimir manage to attend?

AOIFE: He certainly did. It says here your husband's in one of the mourning coaches. He came to see you before you died. With a bunch of roses as big as himself.

COUNTESS MARKIEVICZ: Good old Casi. Extravagant as the Taj Mahal. He'd polish his boots with champagne if he could.

AOIFE: He sounds like a bit of craic.

COUNTESS MARKIEVICZ: Indeed. But no interest in

revolution, unfortunately. We drifted apart, rather. (*Rubs forehead*). Could I be under an anaesthetic? I've heard about people having the most vivid hallucinations during surgery.

AOIFE: I'm afraid you're dead and buried, Countess. You're lying in the Republican Plot in Glasnevin, surrounded by people you used to know. De Valera, Collins, Casement, Cathal Brugha, The O'Rahilly – it's a top-of-the-range line-up. I can call up a picture of your headstone if you like.

COUNTESS MARKIEVICZ: Stop! You're like one of Dickens's monstrous ghosts summoning images from other Christmases. I have no desire to see my headstone. Just supposing what you say is true ...

AOIFE: I know it's a lot to take in, Countess.

COUNTESS MARKIEVICZ: Yes, well, I'm an adaptable person. *Nil desperandum* and so forth. Though do try to remember. You call me 'Madame'. This countessing is rather tiresome.

AOIFE: Sorry. You're my first titled person. I'm a little star-struck.

COUNTESS MARKIEVICZ (*gives regal wave*): *If you prick us, do we not bleed?* I say, how did you convey me here? From wherever I was, I mean?

AOIFE: It was a fluke, really. I knew I needed something you owned for the – well, I don't like to call it a séance. Sounds so spooky. For the process, let's say. '*For best results, an item that belonged to the subject is recommended.*' That's what the online guide to raising the dead said.

COUNTESS MARKIEVICZ: For crying out loud. I've heard some tall tales in my time, but this takes the biscuit. Do you really expect me to believe you engaged in some hocus-pocus and (*clicks fingers*) snapped me back to life?

AOIFE: But that's exactly what happened! Although your

gloves did the trick.

COUNTESS MARKIEVICZ: You're talking in riddles, young woman.

AOIFE: You see, I knew there were exhibits in museums with your hats and revolvers and so on, but museums are unbelievably touchy about lending them out. Unless to other museums. So I went to Lissadell, thinking there might be something I could buy in the gift shop. But there was nothing suitable for raising the dead. Bit of an oversight on the part of their stock-ordering manager, if you ask me. Anyhow, quite by chance, when I was mooching about in Sligo, I came across an old pair of gloves in a charity shop. I'm not sure why I picked them up. They were pretty manky, between you and me. But something told me to take a closer look.

AOIFE *points to the coffee table where a pair of yellowed, elbow-length silk gloves are lying inside a ring of tea-light. The* COUNTESS *stands up and lifts the gloves, examining them.*

COUNTESS MARKIEVICZ: I haven't laid eyes on these since Noah was a boy. Lost them at a soirée in Dublin Castle. Frightful crush. Casi and I took one look and bolted.

AOIFE: I found your initials inside. At least, they're the same as yours. CGB, for Constance Gore-Booth. I took a chance and bought them to use. I think they must have been the clincher. In making the, um, process work. To be honest, I only used the candles for atmosphere. I don't think they advanced the materialisation.

COUNTESS MARKIEVICZ (*lays gloves against her cheek)*: Shabby old things. But you're quite right, they are mine. My sister Eva gave them to me and embroidered my initials inside. How very enterprising of you, my dear.

AOIFE (*claps her hands*): You believe me now!

COUNTESS MARKIEVICZ: I have always made it my business to believe in the impossible. Why not this? So, I'm dead.

What an inconvenience! *(Paces about, slapping the gloves against her palm*). I do hope I didn't conk out in prison. (*All at once she stops walking*). The Free Staters didn't execute me, did they? I know I antagonised them dreadfully. Nearly as much as I riled the British. I was condemned to death after the Rising, you know, by that pompous twerp of a tin soldier General Maxwell. Not only that but he had the cheek to reprieve me, too. Really, I said to the officer communicating the stay of execution, I do wish you chaps would make your minds up, instead of flip-flopping back and forth.

AOIFE: You can't have wanted to face a firing squad!

COUNTESS MARKIEVICZ (no*nchalant shrug)*: I didn't like being treated differently because I was a woman. Mind you, it's something I share in common with Éamon. Being let off, I mean.

AOIFE: Do you mean de Valera?

COUNTESS MARKIEVICZ: *Mr* de Valera to you. I don't think much of your manners in the present day. And do stop biting your nails, my dear girl. My nanny, Squidge, would have rubbed a garlic clove on my fingers if she'd caught me at that. *(Blushing,* AOIFE *jams her hands into the front pockets of her jeans).* Much better for your posture if you stand like this. (*She demonstrates a military at-ease position, hands behind her back.* AOIFE *copies her).* Jolly good show. You're promising material. Would you mind awfully telling me, how did I die?

AOIFE: Don't worry – you weren't shot on the run, or executed by the Free State government, or anything like that. It happened in hospital. Peritonitis, according to the history books.

COUNTESS MARKIEVICZ: I am not in the least bit worried, Miss Blanchard. Information is what I seek, not reassurance. *(Rebukes Aoife with a tap on the forearm).*

AOIFE (*jumps*): *Ouch!* That was weird – it made my stomach flip!

COUNTESS MARKIEVICZ: Yes, a peculiar sensation came over me, too. Chin up. Ride the fear, don't let it ride you. That's what I told my men when we were under machine gun fire from the Shelbourne roof.

AOIFE: How thrilling!

COUNTESS MARKIEVICZ: It was, rather. For about two minutes. Until we realised we were sitting ducks. (*Gnaws lower lip*). I'm starting to remember things. I suppose I must have died in Sir Patrick Dun's. I had a pain in my gut. Ignored it for as long as I could. Said I'd drop in to Kathleen Lynn and have her give me the once-over. But before I could, I passed out. Next thing I remember is waking up in hospital with Éamon de Valera beside my bed. Between you and me, it quite gave me the heebie-jeebies – he looked exactly like an undertaker. Always did. After that, I don't recall anything. What rotten luck! I was counting on an afterlife. Converted to Roman Catholicism to be on the safe side. Ho hum, so much for an eternity of camping trips with my Fianna boys. *(Sits down, squashes her hat).*

AOIFE: I went camping once Never again. Eaten alive by midges.

COUNTESS MARKIEVICZ: They never bothered me.

AOIFE: But nothing bothers you, Madame.

COUNTESS MARKIEVICZ: True. (*Looks* AOIFE *over*). I see from your clothing that women are wearing breeches now. This is normal attire? I approve. Those ill-mannered separation women catcalled about my breeches when we were marched away from the College of Surgeons after the surrender. What larks it would have been to shout back, 'Your granddaughters will be wearing them one day!' Incidentally, young woman, what am I doing here in the future?

AOIFE: I appealed to the universe for you. To ask your advice.

COUNTESS MARKIEVICZ: Proceed.

AOIFE: It's about political representation. Irish women have hardly any. It's utterly depressing. I belong to a group of volunteers working to overturn that.

COUNTESS MARKIEVICZ: I say, good show! Like the Irish Volunteers?

AOIFE: No-oo. We don't drill, or practise shooting. We're not volunteers in a military sense. We're pressing for political change, but progress is unbelievably slow. I thought you might be able to suggest ways to speed it up.

COUNTESS MARKIEVICZ: Have you considered a revolution?

AOIFE: The problem with guns is they just aren't acceptable any more. They create an increased set of risks. The other side always gets its hands on bigger guns and ups the ante. No offence, Madame, I know you were out in 1916.

COUNTESS MARKIEVICZ: No offence taken. Like many revolutionaries, I am a pacifist by nature and inclination. What can I say? Events overtook me. (*Studies the sitting room, furnished from Ikea).* If this is the future, it looks decidedly empty. How many people live here with you?

AOIFE: I live on my own.

COUNTESS MARKIEVICZ: How courageous! But you have a live-in maid, one presumes?

AOIFE: No maid. Couldn't afford one, even if I wanted. Which I don't. I'd feel I was exploiting her. I pay for a cleaning lady now and again.

COUNTESS MARKIEVICZ: But who sets your fires and cooks your meals? Places your weekly order with the butcher and greengrocer? My dear, who answers the door for you?

AOIFE: We have modern conveniences nowadays.

COUNTESS MARKIEVICZ *(scanning the room)*: It doesn't look especially different. (*Picks up an intricately embroidered cushion*). I'm glad to see people still do embroidery. It kept me sane in prison. I was sentenced to hard labour, you know. Scrubbed floors. Sewed nightclothes for prisoners. But I used to pull threads out of the rags they gave me to clean with and save little patches of white cloth from the nightgowns. For embroidery – I think I'd have gone mad with frustration otherwise. Ruins your eyes, of course. Still.

AOIFE: Countess, would it be very rude of me to crack on? The problem is, I don't know how long you're allowed to visit from the other side – there might be a curfew. You could vanish in a puff of smoke when the clock strikes the hour. So, would it be all right if we talked about the reason I called you up?

COUNTESS MARKIEVICZ: Very well.

AOIFE: Let me bring you up to speed. When you were part of the revolution, it looked as though there'd be real political change. I mean to say, you were the first female MP, first female TD, first female minister in Europe – second in the world. It looked as though the old order was about to topple. But the new order was a closed shop, too. With women on the outside. We got the vote. And then, stop right there! Reverse gear engaged!

COUNTESS MARKIEVICZ: Haven't any of your female Taoisigh made a difference?

AOIFE: I'm sorry to say, Countess, I mean Madame, there hasn't been a single, solitary female Taoiseach.

COUNTESS MARKIEVICZ: Not one? Not even one? In an entire century?

AOIFE *(shakes head)*: We've had a few women in the number two slot, but we can't seem to climb any higher than Tánaiste. Fianna Fáil and Fine Gael have never even had a female leader. At least there's pushback now. Women are fed up of being sidelined. Change is finally happening. But the pace is glacial. So I thought if I materialised you, you might have some ideas we could use. To make a breakthrough.

COUNTESS MARKIEVICZ: Disgraceful! The future is quite a disappointment! And to think I was a minister in 1919!

AOIFE: The trailblazing stuttered to a halt, I'm afraid.

COUNTESS MARKIEVICZ: Outrageous! In my day, we believed change was not just inevitable but irreversible. Full equality for all the children of the nation was simply a matter of time. Where did it all go wrong?

AOIFE: Men wouldn't share. They still don't really want to – not in their hearts. The majority, I mean – it's not fair to tar them all with the same brush. After the Anglo-Irish Treaty, that was back in 1921 –

COUNTESS MARKIEVICZ: My dear, I was there, in the thick of it.

AOIFE: Sorry, of course you were. Anyway, a counter-revolution happened. Not all at once, but gradually. Women were exempted from jury service. Banned from state jobs once they got married. Earned less than men when they *could* work. There was no contraception, which didn't help. Basically, women were forced out of public life and back into the home.

COUNTESS MARKIEVICZ: But homelife is so dreary! I mean it's all right in short bursts. But imagine being stuck in it!

AOIFE: Exactly what my mum says.

COUNTESS MARKIEVICZ: Are married women still corralled into the home?

AOIFE: Not so much. We have the same legal rights as men now. Barriers to education have gone. Except money is still an obstacle. Whether you're a woman or a man. We're entitled to the same pay for the same work. In principle, anyhow. But promotion? That's slow. Leadership roles? That's an overreach. They keep telling us they'll give us opportunities to lead if we're good enough. But we never seem to be.

COUNTESS MARKIEVICZ: Damn and blast! How infuriating! I didn't risk bullets for a two-tier Ireland! What kind of man is your current Taoiseach?

AOIFE: Photogenic. Media savvy. Handsome.

COUNTESS MARKIEVICZ: Handsome is as handsome does. Is he kind? Hardworking? Effective? It's a frightful waste to have a duffer as Taoiseach.

AOIFE: I wouldn't call him a duffer, and I'm sure he does work hard. As for being kind, I can't say one way or the other.

COUNTESS MARKIEVICZ: Kindness is an obligation on all of us. Everyone should be a little kinder than we truly care to be. I learned that during the Lockout, running a soup kitchen at Liberty Hall. I suppose you don't need them anymore.

AOIFE: Actually, we do. We still have soup kitchens. And homeless people.

COUNTESS MARKIEVICZ: What? Did Britain invade us again?

AOIFE: No, we're a republic. Since 1949.

COUNTESS MARKIEVICZ: How splendid! That's news worth rising from the dead to hear. But wait – if we rule ourselves, why are Irish people still hungry? That's not the Éire I dreamed about and worked for with James Connolly and all the others.

AOIFE: I'm afraid there's a great deal of unfinished

business, Madame.

COUNTESS MARKIEVICZ: Indeed. (*Leans against the mantelpiece, meditating. By and by, she raises her head*). At least there's been reintegration with the North by now, I presume?

AOIFE: The six North-Eastern counties are still in Northern Ireland.

COUNTESS MARKIEVICZ: You mean to tell me partition hasn't been overturned? (AOIFE *pulls a sad face.* COUNTESS MARKIEVICZ *buries her face in her hands. A muffled voice emerges*). Let's not be daunted. We must focus on continuing the good fight. (*Takes away her hands, inhales, squares her shoulders*). The hand of friendship must be extended to our Unionist brethren. Rome wasn't built in a day. On second thoughts, perhaps I oughtn't to mention Rome and Unionism in the same breath. Riles them up, don't you know. (*Wheels about, eyes alight*). I have a topping idea, young woman. You could try a hunger strike. Always a useful tool, in my experience.

AOIFE: People die on hunger strike!

COUNTESS MARKIEVICZ: If you believe in a cause, you must be willing to do whatever it takes to advance it. Sacrifices will have to be made. There's no alternative.

AOIFE: But a hunger strike is way too radical!

COUNTESS MARKIEVICZ: Do you suppose I said to myself 'revolutions are too radical' when I buckled up and reported for duty on Easter Monday?

AOIFE: I'm grateful for your suggestion, Madame. Truly I am. But is there any chance you'd have a Plan B?

COUNTESS MARKIEVICZ: I must say your lack of grit is disappointing. If you're representative of the calibre of women today, it doesn't inspire much confidence.

AOIFE: Sorry to be so hopeless. That's why we need your

help, Countess. We're throwing ourselves on your mercy.

COUNTESS MARKIEVICZ: Oh, very well. But call me Madame. Now, let me think. (*Lifts hat, twirls on fingers).* I have it! Women must become activists again. Take the suffrage movement as your model. You should run a campaign along suffragette lines. They understood how to be effective. Here's what you do. Heckle senior politicians in public. Chain yourself to the Leinster House railings. Make placards and banners. Go on marches with them. Blowing whistles. They'll loathe that. The ruling class has no tolerance for noise, except when they're making it. I learned that in the nursery. Old Squidge was always telling us, *stop causing a disturbance.* Mama and Papa were fixated on silence. I expect your Taoiseach and his Cabinet like everything nice and quiet, too.

AOIFE: I suppose we could try some rallies. We've been too ladylike. Asked politely for our rights instead of demanding them.

COUNTESS MARKIEVICZ: If I may say so, Miss Blanchard, it sounds as if you've grown complacent. In my day, we didn't mind raising a row. If you want something badly enough, forget about the courtesies. The time for being genteel is long past.

AOIFE: I think my generation has just forgotten how to protest in person. We think we can do it all online.

COUNTESS MARKIEVICZ: A dash of turbulence never goes amiss. I remember the time the suffragettes filled their pockets with stones and broke windows the length and breadth of Kildare Street.

AOIFE (*gulps*): Wouldn't that lead to a court appearance?

COUNTESS MARKIEVICZ: And your point is? *(Impatient, pushes hair back from face).* Dramatic public gestures direct attention to a cause. They attract criticism, of course, but they also draw in converts.

AOIFE: I don't want to seem like a total wuss, Madame –

COUNTESS MARKIEVICZ: Puss?

AOIFE: No, wuss. It's a coward. But I can't see my committee agreeing to a stone-throwing campaign. You could put someone's eye out. Besides, it's illegal.

COUNTESS MARKIEVICZ: Fiddlesticks! What a tame lot you are. You need to nail your colours to the mast. If you genuinely believe in something, it's worth fighting for. Whatever the cost. When the Irish nation was conjured into being, we trusted it would mean equality for all. You can't let some self-centred men get away with scaling down the revolution. You must organise. Strategise. Agitate! Centre your campaign around a mass movement of women. Here's what you do – call a women's strike. Have all your female followers withdraw their labour from the workplace and the home. That won't go unnoticed, believe me.

AOIFE: I'm not sure we have the support for action on that scale.

The COUNTESS *grasps* AOIFE *by the shoulders, only to drop her hands at once. Both of them shiver.*

COUNTESS MARKIEVICZ: I keep forgetting I shouldn't touch you. But I want to shake you, my dear, honestly I do. What are you, women or cry-babies? Stand up for your rights – nobody will serve them to you on a bone-china dinner plate! You're educated. With opportunities women could only fantasise about in my day, from what you say. You must use your collective strength. Show the Government you have a grievance and don't be afraid to make yourselves disagreeable until you have what's rightfully yours. (*Slaps dent out of hat, jams on her head).* I shall meet this Taoiseach of yours and give him a piece of my mind. Let us find an omnibus stop and pay him a call immediately.

AOIFE: You can't just arrive on the Taoiseach's doorstep, Madame.

COUNTESS MARKIEVICZ: We'll see about that. I'd like to meet the minion who'll stop me!

AOIFE: What will you say to the Taoiseach?

COUNTESS MARKIEVICZ: That inequality wrapped in the flag of a republic remains just that. Inequality. Shape up, my man, I'll tell him. And if he tries to give me any lip, he'll be sorry. I'm too long in the tooth to take it from any man.

AOIFE: I shouldn't think he'll give you any lip, Madame. Actually, I have it on good authority he has lovely manners.

COUNTESS MARKIEVICZ: Never mind that old courtesy palaver. I don't want men standing up when I enter a room, I want them listening to what I have to say – that's the best kind of respect. Not fetching our wraps and escorting us to tea parties. Frankly, my dear, I find it vexatious to be dragged into the twenty-first century – without my Poppet for company – to deal with your Taoiseach. But deal with him I shall. *(Hands on hip).* I faced down a court martial of army officers drunk with blood lust. I faced down officious prison governors and their meddlesome warders. I faced down former comrades when they chose a different path and the country was plunged into civil war. A Taoiseach holds no terrors for me.

AOIFE: You're magnificent!

COUNTESS MARKIEVICZ: No hero worship, if you please! It's unseemly. Fetch my coat. Oh, I didn't bring one from the afterlife. Very well, let us go as we are. Follow me.

AOIFE: Where to?

COUNTESS MARKIEVICZ: The Taoiseach's office! Where else?

AOIFE (*wrings hands)*: Is this wise? I don't even know if you can go outside, Madame. What if daylight shrivels you up? What if you turn to dust?

COUNTESS MARKIEVICZ: I am not a vampire. I am a revolutionary. Chop-chop, time's a-wasting. Fall in! Left-right, left-right!

AOIFE *marches into place behind her.* AOIFE *and* COUNTESS MARKIEVICZ *march off stage.*

Act Two

Outside the Department of the Taoiseach, Upper Merrion Street, Dublin.

AOIFE: So, here we are. That's the Taoiseach's office through those gates.

COUNTESS MARKIEVICZ: Cosgrave's lot thought they had permanent rights to the place. Most infuriating. Bunch of milk-and-water clerks the lot of them. *(To the security guard watching them).* Kindly open the gate, my man. I have business to attend to.

GUARD (*folds his arms, facing her down*): I don't care if you're the Queen of Sheba, you can't come in here without a pass.

COUNTESS MARKIEVICZ: I am a former Minister for Labour. I have earned permanent access to the seat of government.

GUARD: Show us your ID, missis.

COUNTESS MARKIEVICZ: It's 'Madame' to you. I don't appear to have a calling card about my person. Nor should I require one. My name is my calling card. Kindly inform the Taoiseach that Madame de Markievicz requests an appointment.

GUARD: Is he expecting you?

COUNTESS MARKIEVICZ: He is not. Nevertheless, I insist on seeing him. If he is a gentleman, he will not refuse me.

GUARD: No seeing the boss without an appointment. He's a busy man.

COUNTESS MARKIEVICZ: And I am a busy woman. I have travelled an extremely long way to see him, thanks to the ingenuity of this young person beside me, Miss Aoife Blanchard. Now, I insist on you informing the

Taoiseach's people that I am waiting.

GUARD: Will he know who you are?

COUNTESS MARKIEVICZ: My name ought to ring a bell. (*Whispers loudly to Aoife*). Perhaps I ought not to presume?

AOIFE: He'll know you, Madame, you're on the school curriculum. And there's a bust of you in The Green. Oh, and a statue in Townsend Street. You haven't been forgotten.

COUNTESS MARKIEVICZ: How topping! Would it be too conceited to go and inspect them after I've finished with the Taoiseach? I do hope they've spelled Markievicz correctly.

AOIFE: I'm sure it's right. We have spellcheck now. You'll like the Townsend Street statue. There's a little dog at your ankles.

COUNTESS MARKIEVICZ: I say, I wonder if it's Poppet? How kind of the sculptor. Really, it's not much of an afterlife without my spaniel. Or even my Fianna boys. Actually, I wish I could remember what the afterlife *is* like. It's all a frightful blur.

GUARD *(makes flapping gesture)*: That's enough gabbing. I need yous to leave right now.

COUNTESS MARKIEVICZ: Kindly be silent. I'm thinking.

GUARD: Yous can do your thinking someplace else. Government property's no place for thinking.

COUNTESS MARKIEVICZ: You will not batter me into submission, you bully. I am staying put.

GUARD: Nobody's laying a finger on you, missis. I'm only asking you politely for to leave the premises.

COUNTESS MARKIEVICZ: Politely? I was treated with more courtesy by Captain de Courcy-Wheeler when I yielded my gun to him!

GUARD: Jaysus, do you have a gun on you? Where's the law when you need it? *(Takes whistle from pocket and blows. Shouts*). Emergency! Guards! I need some guards over here!

COUNTESS MARKIEVICZ: Such poppycock. I am unarmed, my man. Stop putting words in my mouth. And kindly put that ridiculous whistle away. What a panicker you are. I'm very glad I didn't have you in my unit in the College of Surgeons.

AOIFE: We don't have any guns, I promise. We're pacifists. (*Casts anxious glance at* COUNTESS*).* At least, you are now, isn't that right, Madame?

COUNTESS MARKIEVICZ: There are no weapons in the afterlife. Besides, as I told you, I was forced to surrender my Mauser to Captain de Courcy-Wheeler. He was on General Maxwell's staff. Remind me, later, to ask you what happened to that butcher. Bloody Maxwell, we called him. *(Curls lip).* I presume the British heaped him with honours and gave him a seat in the House of Lords.

Just then, TAOISEACH *appears in a tracksuit, a towel around his neck. He jogs to one side and starts doing warm-up stretches.*

AOIFE: Madame, that's him! *(Tugs* COUNTESS *by sleeve.* COUNTESS *has her back to* TAOISEACH*).* The Taoiseach!

COUNTESS MARKIEVICZ *(turns around, does a double take)*: Really? That's your Taoiseach?

TAOISEACH *rubs his face with the towel.*

COUNTESS MARKIEVICZ *(takes a step backwards):* Good grief, he's treating the street as though it's his bathroom.

AOIFE: You mean the towel? That's just for his jog. Sweaty business, jogging. If you do it right.

COUNTESS MARKIEVICZ: A Taoiseach who sweats! And dresses for bed in the middle of the day! Why on earth is he wearing pyjamas? Hasn't he any work to do?

The TAOISEACH *takes off his zip-up jogging top and turns away from the audience. He's wearing a t-shirt with 'Campaign for Leo' in large letters on the back.*

AOIFE: I expect so. But they say he's mad into keep-fit. Always at the gym.

COUNTESS MARKIEVICZ*:* Who, might one inquire, is Jim?

AOIFE: It's a place where people do exercises. To fight the flab. Government ministers have to do a lot of dining out for Ireland.

The TAOISEACH *starts running on the spot, while singing a Kylie Minogue song.*

TAOISEACH (*singing*): 'I should be so lucky, lucky, lucky, lucky, I should be lucky in love.' (*Stops running, pants*). We'll soon see about that metabolic age. *(Begins doing chest expansion exercises).*

COUNTESS MARKIEVICZ (*gapes at him*): Such nonsense! He should go on manoeuvres with my Fianna boys if he wants some healthy exercise. Yomp about the Sally Gap with a pack on his back. That'd trim his sails for him.

The TAOISEACH *goes to move off.* COUNTESS MARKIEVICZ *stands in front of him.*

COUNTESS MARKIEVICZ *(raises hand)*: Halt! I have a bone to pick with you.

TAOISEACH *(high-fives her):* Hi there, good to meet you.

COUNTESS MARKIEVICZ (*stares at her palm, shrugs*): Good day to you. My name is Constance de Markievicz and I have returned from the dead to tell you that the women of Ireland are extremely disappointed in you.

TAOISEACH: A, I don't believe in ghosts, and B, I'm a feminist. I like women. So fair's fair, they should like me.

COUNTESS MARKIEVICZ: A, I don't care whether you believe

in me or not – the important thing is *I* believe in me. And B, we're indifferent to being liked. We want you to give us our due. Your government needs more women on the inside, making decisions. Time's up on that selfish boys' club you're running.

TAOISEACH: Is this a candid camera setup? *(Looks around for a lens).* Oh wait, I have it. You're one of those 1916 actors off the tour buses, aren't you? *(Laughs).* I have to hand it to you – you look exactly like her. We could use you for our party *árd fheis*. You'd be a super interval act. Have your people speak to my people.

COUNTESS MARKIEVICZ: That's enough of your impertinence! Resist the impudence to call me an actor. Or to suggest using me as an – an – interval act! This isn't the music hall.

TAOISEACH *(fiddles with mobile phone in his hand)*: Tell you what, why don't we do a selfie? Then I'll have to press on. Work's piling up. I still haven't recorded my weekly address to the Irish people. Hashtag #politicsmeets pizzazz. And I really need to fit in some jogging.

COUNTESS MARKIEVICZ: I haven't the foggiest notion what a selfie is. Nor will I be diverted by your reference to it. And kindly desist from fidgeting with that object in your hand while I address you.

TAOISEACH: You sound a lot like my mum when you use that tone.

COUNTESS MARKIEVICZ: A worthy woman, no doubt. We shall invite the good lady to join our struggle.

TAOISEACH: Not sure I like the idea of a struggle.

COUNTESS MARKIEVICZ: Ah, but there's rapture in the struggle!

GUARD: Here, none of that. *An Taoiseach* has a full itinerary and there's no space for rapture in it.

COUNTESS MARKIEVICZ: Have the common courtesy not to

butt in. You are not party to this conversation. I presume, Taoiseach, you can spare the time to discuss the Irish Republic – which is failing to live up to its potential.

TAOISEACH: We're a work in progress. Brexit's the problem. We're so busy future-proofing it, *(shrugs, extends hands)* we've no time left for the present. But trust me. It's gonna be great. I have full confidence in my government's ability to –

COUNTESS MARKIEVICZ *(interrupts)*: Enough! Taoiseach, you have won a place in history. But if you want history to look kindly on you, you need to show you've earned that place.

The TAOISEACH *gives her a considering look, taking her seriously now.*

TAOISEACH: What do you have in mind?

COUNTESS MARKIEVICZ: Cancel your appointments for the day. You and I have a great deal to thrash out.

TAOISEACH: Sorry, logistics. Impossible.

COUNTESS MARKIEVICZ: Don't bandy logistics at me. We'd never have stood out for the best part of a week against the might of the British Empire without some grasp of logistics.

TAOISEACH: Suppose I might be able to squeeze you in for some face time towards the end of next week.

COUNTESS MARKIEVICZ: Look here, I haven't a clue where I'll be next week. Has nobody instructed you in the merits of *carpe diem*? Do you, or don't you, want future generations to remember you as a visionary Taoiseach?

TAOISEACH *(checks diary on phone)*: Guess I could spare you half an hour now if I cut short my jog. All right, let's do it. It'll only take me a minute to change. Come with me. *(To the guard)*. Let her through, please.

He extends his hand to the COUNTESS, *inviting her to precede him.*

COUNTESS MARKIEVICZ *(over her shoulder to* AOIFE*)*: You were quite right, my dear. His manners do him credit. Even if his policies need work.

AOIFE *(calls after her)*: Madame, will I wait here for you? *(To* GUARD*)*. Oh dear, I don't think she heard me. I hope she'll be ok.

GUARD *(throws eyes heavenwards)*: No better wan! She's some piece of work. Here, now that it's just the two of us, you can tell me. I know she was acting up for the boss, but she *is* off one of them there tour buses? Isn't she?

AOIFE: Why can't she be who she says she is?

GUARD *snorts, withdrawing into his hut.*

AOIFE (*turns to audience and smiles)*: Countess Markievicz. In the flesh.

ACKNOWLEDGEMENTS

The author and publisher wish to thank historian and publisher Mícheál Ó Doibhilín of Kilmainham Tales, Teo, for kind permission to reproduce the poster of Countess Markievicz he designed for the 1916 Relatives Association.

Thanks also to Lia Mills and Simon Robinson for tracking down Countess Markievicz's London home with me.

And thank you Margaret Dunne, of Dalkey Castle & Heritage Centre, for first suggesting that *What Would The Countess Say?* should be staged – and making it happen.

About the Author

Martina Devlin is an author, journalist and playwright. She has written eight novels, two non-fiction books, two plays and a short story collection. Her latest work is *Edith: A Novel* about *The Irish R.M.* writer Edith Somerville. Prizes include the Royal Society of Literature's V.S. Pritchett Prize and a Hennessy Literary Award. She writes a weekly current affairs column for the *Irish Independent* and has been named National Newspapers of Ireland commentator of the year. Martina hosts the City of Books podcast for Dublin UNESCO City of Literature. She is the first holder of a Ph.D. in literary practice from Trinity College Dublin, where she has lectured on Irish literature.

More information www.martinadevlin.ie